CHRIST ILLUMINATED

SEEING JESUS FOR WHO HE IS

JOY MARGETTS

Be blessed!

Joy x

kevin mayhew

First Published in 2023 by Kevin Mayhew Ltd,

Fengate Farm,

Rattlesden,

Bury St Edmunds,

Suffolk, IP30 0SZ

ISBN (paperback): 9781838581855

ISBN (eBook): 9781838581862

Paperback product code: 1501736

eBook product code: 1501737

CONTENTS

Endorsements v
About the Author ix
Introduction xi

Part I
WONDERFUL COUNSELLOR
Day 1 3
Day 2 6
Day 3 9
Day 4 12
Day 5 15
Day 6 18
Reflection 21

Part II
PRINCE OF PEACE
Day 7 25
Day 8 28
Day 9 31
Day 10 34
Day 11 37
Day 12 40
Reflection 43

Part III
MIGHTY GOD, EVERLASTING FATHER
Day 13 47
Day 14 50
Day 15 53
Day 16 56
Day 17 59
Day 18 62
Reflection 65

Part IV
FOR UNTO US A CHILD IS BORN, UNTO US A SON IS GIVEN

Day 19 69
Day 20 72
Day 21 75
Day 22 78
Day 23 81
Day 24 84
Reflection 87
Love Incarnate 88

Acknowledgements 89

ENDORSEMENTS

If you buy only one devotional to follow this Advent, I heartily recommend this one.

Christ Illuminated does exactly as the title suggests, shedding light on the nature and character of Jesus, the centre of our celebrations.

Joy Margetts' gentle voice guides us through His many names with care and passion. Her writing follows rabbinic tradition by holding each scripture up to the light like a jewel, so we can appreciate different facets of the whole. Her thoughtful, provocative questions, beautiful prayers and helpful reflections will call you, as they did me, into a deeper walk with God. Be prepared to be challenged, and allow God to meet you in a place of vulnerability and faith as you press in to Him this Christmas.

May this devotional serve as a refuge amidst the bustle and noise around you; and mayyou know again the wonder of the season as you allow the magnificence of our Saviour to embrace you.

— JENNY SANDERS; SPEAKER AND AUTHOR OF *SPIRITUAL FEASTING* AND *POLISHED ARROWS* (SPRING 2024)

Joy's devotional is rich with the Word of God. She writes with a prophetic edge drawing us into the Advent season in a Spirit-led and timely manner that ministers and challenges me deep in my soul.

Her questions apply the Scripture in a way that causes reflection long after they have been read.

If you desire to go deeper with Jesus this is an incredible tool.

__ ANNE CALVER; SPEAKER, AUTHOR AND PIONEER OF *UNLEASHED*

This book is like a casket full of treasures, each day showing a different beautiful aspect of who Jesus is. It is not just a book of theories *about* Him, but offers daily invitations to deepen our relationship *with* Him - the greatest treasure of all! Readers will surely be blessed as they draw closer to Jesus this Advent through the riches contained in these pages.

__ RACHEL YARWORTH; AUTHOR OF *FRIEND OF GOD: THE MIRACULOUS LIFE OF AN ORDINARY PERSON* AND *THE JESSE TREE ANTHOLOGY*

I have read many advent devotionals and love how they focus my mind on why we are celebrating Christmas, so I was excited to start reading Joy Margetts', *Christ Illuminated -Seeing Jesus for who He is.* I discovered immediately how apt that title is - every reading, in fact, every sentence illuminates the person of Jesus: who He is, His heart of love and all He came to do for us. Rooted in Scripture and with an engaging, easy to read style, Joy takes us on a treasure hunt revealing the depth and richness of Jesus' many names and attributes. I found her invitations to reflect - *Ask Yourself; Ask God;* and *Pray* at the end of each devotional a wonderful means of growing in my love of Jesus.

It is such a beautiful, life-giving resource that can be used not just at Advent but anytime and can be read alone or as part of a study group. I found it thrilling to have my eyes opened afresh to who Jesus is and am excited to continue that journey of discovery. Thank you Joy!

__ TRACY WILLIAMSON; AUTHOR AND SPEAKER WITH MBM TRUST – RESTORING LIVES THROUGH INTIMACY WITH GOD

As if examining a multi-faceted diamond, Joy Margetts takes us to some of the many and varied descriptions of the Lord Jesus Christ, exposing their beauty and relevance for the Christmas season. Ideal in length for a daily devotion and winsomely applied with helpful questions.

__ ANDY PATERSON

ABOUT THE AUTHOR

Joy Margetts is the author of several Christian historical fiction books. She loves history but is even more passionate about the Word of God. She teaches regularly in local church and has a heart to point people towards Jesus and the reality of His Kingdom in all of her writing.

Joy is a mother and grandmother and makes her home on the beautiful North Wales Coast. More about Joy and her writing can be found on her website www.joymargetts.com.

INTRODUCTION

Advent is a special time. We look forward with expectancy to Christmas Day, and the celebrations we will have. We think of the loved ones we might share Christmas with, in the giving of gifts, and in food and fun. We look forward to time away from work, school, or the other pressures on our time. We get excited by the colourful decorations appearing in streets and homes. We see the joy in the faces of children as they anticipate all that Christmas brings.

But Christmas is about Jesus. The celebrations are for His birthday. And we do celebrate Him with our carols and our special services. But what if we took time, every day, in the weeks of Advent to focus, just for a few minutes on Jesus - on who He is and what He came to earth to accomplish? And what better way to do that than to look at the names Jesus is given in the Bible, the way the Word of God describes Him.

These thoughts of mine were originally published as short 'blogs' but, in revisiting them for the purposes of this publication, I have added to them. Each devotional thought is, to the best of my ability, well grounded in Scripture. Where I have added to the Word of God is in an attempt to make the

Word applicable. Following each devotional thought is an invitation to meditate on what the name or descriptor of Jesus means to you personally. There are things to ask yourself, and things to ask God. And a prayer for you to pray if it helps. My prayer is that this format really blesses you, and allows the Holy Spirit to apply what you have read to your own personal experience of Jesus.

There are many, many ways in which Jesus is described in the Bible. The names and descriptors I have chosen are mostly familiar, with a few more obscure ones thrown in. My desire is that these devotionals help you to see Jesus in all His fullness. I believe very strongly that the Old Testament, as well as the New Testament, speaks of Jesus. All the Old Testament prophecies I have used are ones that I believe refer quite clearly to the coming Messiah, and they are almost all referenced to or quoted by New Testament writers. They may have meant something else to the people who first read them, but in the light of Christ's coming, I believe that we can see that God inspired those ancient writers to speak of, and point ahead to, His Son. All of them I believe will help us prepare our hearts for Christmas.

The book is divided into four sections, each consisting of six daily devotionals. I have arranged it this way so that the devotional can be used as a daily aid for the twenty-four days of December, or as a weekly devotional, corresponding to the four weeks of Advent. At the beginning of each section is a short introduction, and at the end of each section an invitation to reflect back on the previous six days. In this way the devotional could be used as a personal study guide, or you and a friend (or friends) could work through it together and share your thoughts at the end of each section.

Isaiah 9:6-7 is a familiar scripture often read around Christmas. In it the prophet declares that a son is going to be given, a child born, '*And His Name will be called…*'

For unto us a Child is born,
Unto us a Son is given;
And the government will be upon His shoulder.
And His name will be called
Wonderful, Counselor, Mighty God,
Everlasting Father, Prince of Peace.
Isaiah 9:6 NKJV

I have taken this scripture as the framework for all the devotionals that follow. Each section is based on a name, or names, given to us by Isaiah in this prophecy. Section 1 looks at Jesus as our 'Wonderful Counsellor' - how He came as a man, and knows and provides all that we need. In the scripture reference above there is a comma after 'Wonderful'; a comma that isn't there in other versions. That Jesus is wonderful is without question, but for the purposes of this devotional I have chosen to combine the two names into the more familiar 'Wonderful Counsellor ' and to use the English spelling for 'counselor'.

Section 2 looks at Jesus as our 'Prince of Peace' - the long promised Messianic King who brought with Him a kingdom of peace. Section 3 looks at Jesus our 'Mighty God' and 'Everlasting Father' - focussing on the divinity of Jesus. And Section 4 looks at Isaiah's introduction to this prophecy, 'Unto us a Child is born, Unto us a Son is given'. This final section focusses on the Christmas story and the incarnation of Christ.

I believe that in using this book 'Christ Illuminated: Seeing Jesus for who He really is' we can have our hearts and minds opened to appreciate in a deeper and more insightful way, how wonderful our Saviour is. And perhaps it will enable us to trust Him more fully, love Him more deeply, and worship Him more wholeheartedly this Christmas.

PART I

WONDERFUL COUNSELLOR

AND HIS NAME SHALL BE CALLED...

Jesus is all that we need.
He is the source of our spiritual life and food for our souls.
He is the foundation stone safe enough to build our lives upon.
He is the one who makes us fruitful and the light by which we live in a dark world.
Jesus knows what we need and how to provide it for us, because He lived on earth as one of us.
And yet He is still God.
He is our Wonderful Counsellor, the One who loves to come alongside us.

DAY 1

THE SON OF MAN

"For even the Son of Man did not come to be served, but to serve, and to give His life a ransom for many."
Mark 10:45 NKJV

How did Jesus refer to Himself? With a title used more frequently than any other given Him in scripture. According to biblical scholars He refers to Himself in the Gospels as the 'Son of Man' seventy-eight times. It is significant that Jesus chose to associate Himself with mankind in this way, rather than calling Himself the 'Son of God'. He who created humanity, loved human beings so much that He chose to humble Himself to come to earth to live among us, to experience life as we do and to ultimately die for us. Jesus describes Himself, the Son of Man, as coming not *'to be served but to serve, and to give His life a ransom for many'* (Mark 10:45).

In Mark's gospel Jesus also describes the Son of Man as having the power to forgive sins (Mark 2:10), something that only God can do, and that the Son of Man is also *'Lord of the*

Sabbath' (Mark 2:28). Even though He came as the Son of Man, Jesus also claimed divinity. He tells his followers that the Son of Man will suffer and die (Mark 8:31), will rise from the dead (Mark 9:9), will one day return (Mark 13:26), and that He will sit in judgement with the Father (Mark 8:38).

Jesus was not using the title 'Son of Man' just to emphasise His humanity, but also because of a prophecy in Daniel 7. Daniel saw an image of the *'Ancient of Days'* (God the Father) seated on His throne (v9). Someone else is then brought into the heavenly throne room – *'one like the Son of Man'* (v13). It is to Him that all glory and dominion over the nations of the world are given, a Kingdom that will last forever (v14). This is an image of the exalted Christ, prophesied hundreds of years before Jesus even walked on the earth, and a familiar prophecy to those of Jesus' time who were awaiting their Messiah. They knew that when Jesus used the term 'Son of Man' He was claiming to be the One they were waiting for.

John's vision in Revelation 5:6 -14 echoes Daniel's vision. The Lamb is brought forward before the throne of God, as the only one worthy to take the scroll, because He was slain for the redemption of mankind. To the Lamb is given all the glory and honour and praise, forever and ever.

Jesus, the Son of Man, came as the servant of humanity. He took on our humanness, and gave His very life for our salvation. But the 'Son of Man' is also the forever exalted Lamb of God worthy of our eternal praise. The King of Kings and Lord of Lords.

Ask Yourself: *Do I love humanity like Jesus does, and am I willing to humble myself to serve others in a way that reveals His love?*

Ask God: *Show me, Jesus, any areas of my life where I do not recognise you as King of Kings and Lord of Lords.*

Pray: *Thank You Jesus that You came to earth as the Son of Man, to associate Yourself with us, to live among us, and to die for us. Thank You that because of Your willingness to humble Yourself, even to death on the cross, that I can know You as my Lord and Saviour. Thank You that You are now the exalted One, standing at the right hand of the Father in heaven. You are worthy of all of my praise, forever and ever.*

Help me to serve others as You did, out of the overflow of Your love for me. Help me to make You Lord of every area of my life, which is what You deserve.

Amen.

Further Reading: Daniel 7:1, 9-14

DAY 2

FOUNTAIN OF LIFE

"In that day a fountain shall be opened for the house of David and for the inhabitants of Jerusalem, for sin and for uncleanness."
Zechariah 13:1 NKJV

The little book of Zechariah is full of Messianic prophecies. The one in Zechariah 13:1 promises a *'fountain'* for the house of David. The explicit purpose for this fountain is for cleansing from sin. If we turn to Psalm 36:9 the Psalmist declares that it is God Himself who is the *'fountain of life'*. Jesus, as God incarnate, came into the world to be a fountain - the source of eternal life, cleansing and healing.

Now when we read the word 'fountain' we might think of an ornamental stone fountain placed in a grand garden. The fountain spoken of here is something completely different. The word 'fountain' could be translated as 'spring' but that is not enough if all we picture is a trickling flow of water on a rocky mountainside. This fountain is more, much more - it springs up and flows over in torrents, a constant flow of never-ending water, a wellspring full of life and cleansing. Soaking. Drenching.

When He walked the earth Jesus chose to pass through Samaria so that He could meet a woman who had gone alone and ashamed to draw water from the village well. He knew what she needed. She needed to be cleansed and forgiven and given a new start, and so Jesus begins a discussion with her about water and life. He tells her that it is He Himself who is the source of water that will satisfy her thirst forever, and that the water He gives will become like a fountain of life within her (John 4:14). All she needs to do is to 'drink' what He is offering her, to believe He is who He says He is and find new, eternal life in Him. To drink of that fountain of life is still on offer to all of us, if we are thirsty enough. Jesus invites us still to come and drink (Revelation 21:6).

In the natural world, water is necessary for life. As human beings living in the developed world we have the blessing of being able to turn a tap on at any time and access a clean, constant water source for drinking and cleansing. In the spiritual, Jesus is that water source. He is the source of all spiritual life, creating life within us and sustaining that life. He offers cleansing - because He shed His blood we can be washed, made white as snow (Isaiah 1:18) if we come to Him repentant. And we can do that at any time.

So next time you turn on the tap for water, take a moment to connect with the One who is the ever-flowing fountain of life and thank Him for your life in Him. Whenever you need forgiveness and cleansing, whenever you feel dry and thirsty, He offers the water of life - His life-giving Spirit (Revelation 22:17).

***Ask Yourself**: Do I automatically go to Jesus, the fountain of life, when I need refreshing, or do I look to other sources to satisfy my thirst?*

***Ask God**: Show me, Jesus, any areas of my life where I need the cleansing of Your life-giving water and give me the grace to come to You to ask for your forgiveness.*

***Pray:** Thank You Jesus that You are the fountain of life and that You still offer Yourself to all who come to You thirsty and repentant. Thank you that You are the source of life and like water from the tap, always available to me when I need spiritual refreshing or cleansing. Thank You that the fountain of life is a never-ending flowing stream within those who belong to You.*

Jesus, help me to come to You to drink deeply when I feel dry and not to look to other sources to satisfy my thirst. As You have cleansed me, and continue to cleanse me, I bring to You those who still need to take their first drink of Your life-giving water. Those who still need to find forgiveness and new life in You. Help them to see You for who You are, and to believe in You.

Thank you Jesus.

Amen.

Further Reading: John 4:1-26

DAY 3

BREAD OF LIFE

And Jesus said to them, "I am the bread of life. He who comes to Me shall never hunger, and he who believes in Me shall never thirst."
John 6:35 NKJV

In John 6:1-13 we read the story of how Jesus miraculously fed the 5,000. Barely a day later Jesus is being mobbed by a crowd demanding that this 'magician' do another miracle for them (John 6:30-31). They try and spiritualise their request by referring to the manna, or bread from heaven, that God had sent to feed the Israelites in the desert (Exodus 16). Jesus' reply is that they need to look for the true bread from heaven (John 6:32-33). He knew that they were looking to satisfy their natural desires, but that they needed to be much more concerned with the food that would give them eternal life.

'I am the bread of life,' He tells them, *'He who comes to Me shall never hunger'* (John 6:35). What stands before them, what is on offer to them, is much more than a miraculous gift of physical bread, but the very source of eternal life. He urges them to feed

on Him. He is the living bread, sent from heaven to satisfy every need and desire of their hearts (John 6:48-51).

Now, I love bread. It is the hardest thing for me to give up when trying to lose weight! There is nothing so tempting as a fresh loaf of crusty bread, warm from the oven. It looks good and smells wonderful, but if I just set it on the table in front of you and told you to just look and smell, that would be cruel! Bread is to be eaten.

The Bread of Life is the same. Jesus urges us to feed on Him, to have every spiritual and emotional need met. How? Well in the same way as we ingest bread, we need to take Him into ourselves. First, we invite Him to be Lord of our lives, invite Him into our hearts, and accept His gift of eternal life. But then, just as the Israelites needed daily manna, so we need to feast on Him daily, by spending time talking with Him, worshipping Him, and reading and meditating on His word. He is the only thing that can feed our spiritual lives and keep us healthy, strong and growing.

Jesus left us an invitation when He inaugurated the Lord's Supper on the night He was betrayed. He broke the bread and offered it to His disciples, and said, 'Take eat, this is my body broken for you' (1 Corinthians 11:23-24). Every time we celebrate that love feast the broken bread helps us to remember that it was His death that bought our life. But the invitation to 'take, eat' is not just reserved for those times when we share communion. He invites us to feed from Him, the Living Bread, every day of our lives.

***Ask Yourself**: Do I accept Jesus's invitation to feed on Him daily? What happens when I don't?*

Ask God: Show me, Jesus, what I need to do, to feed on You, the Bread of Life, in the way that is most effective for me.

***Pray:** Thank You Jesus that You willingly gave up Your life, allowing Your body to be broken on the cross, so that I can know You as my living bread. Thank You that You have all that I need to keep me spiritually fed and healthy, every day of my life. Thank You that the bread You offer always satisfies my hunger.*

Help me to be more determined to accept Your invitation to 'take, eat', of the spiritual food that You offer me. Help me to always remember what it cost You, the Bread of Life, to give me life. You are all I need to keep me healthy and strong as I take time to feed on You.

Thank you Jesus.

Amen.

Further Reading: John 6:41-58

DAY 4

CORNERSTONE

Behold, I lay in Zion a stone for a foundation,
A tried stone, a precious cornerstone, a sure foundation;
Isaiah 28:16 NKJV

Isaiah the prophet lived many hundreds of years before Christ was born in Bethlehem. Yet here, in Isaiah 28:16 he looks ahead to One who was to come whom God would set in place as a foundation, a cornerstone, safe and solid to build on. Reading Ephesians 2:20-22 we know that it is Jesus that will become this '*chief cornerstone*'.

A cornerstone would be the first stone laid in any build. It would have to be well cut, have perfect alignment and be secure in its placement. So that whatever was built upon it would also be in perfect alignment and rise up stable and strong.

The promised cornerstone that is Jesus, Isaiah tells us, would be tried (tested) and precious, and would be a sure (trustworthy) foundation. We aren't talking about a small brick here, more like a solid block of unyielding granite that has passed every stress test imaginable and has proved its worth. Jesus passed every test, including the test of the cross, living in perfect obedience to His Father, and so has proved Himself both precious and trustworthy, solid enough to build our lives, and indeed the whole church, on (1 Peter 2:4-6). In Psalm 118:22 we read that this '*chief cornerstone*' would be rejected by those who could not see its worth, but would stand nevertheless.

There is another reference to a stone in Isaiah which points to Jesus. The Messiah will be *'a stone of stumbling and a rock of offense'*, (Isaiah 8:14).

Now a stumbling block is just that - it is large stone that trips you up as you blindly go down a path not looking at where you are putting your feet! It stops you in your tracks and maybe even makes you fall flat on your face. 1 Peter 2:8 makes it clear that it is those who blindly go off down the path of disobedience that will find themselves stumbling on the block that is Jesus. He will make them reconsider the path they are on and where they are headed.

To those who believe, Jesus the Cornerstone is immeasurably precious. His love, His righteousness, and His truth, tested in the fire of suffering, are the surest foundation we could ever need to centre our lives on. The conviction of His Spirit and of His Word, can also be the stumbling block we need, to stop us in our tracks and get us back on the right path when we have wandered.

***Ask Yourself**: Is all that I am building, all that I am working on, firmly built upon the Cornerstone that is Jesus?*

Ask God: *Show me Jesus, through the conviction of Your Spirit and Your Word, which paths I need to stop walking down. Be my stumbling block.*

***Pray:** Jesus, thank You for Your perfect obedience to the Father that brought You to this world as a human child, and ultimately to the Cross for my redemption. Thank You for the example that You set for me, and for the way You love me. Thank You that I can trust You as my sure foundation stone, and also to be my stumbling block when I need You to be. Help me to only ever build what can be securely built on Your truth, and to only walk the paths where You want me to walk. Then I will be strong and secure in You whatever life throws at me.*

Amen.

Further Reading: 1 Peter 2:1-10

DAY 5

THE VINE

"I am the vine, you are the branches.
He who abides in Me, and I in him, bears much fruit; for without Me you can do nothing"
John 15:5 NKJV

In John 15:1 Jesus makes this statement, *'I am the true vine, and My Father is the vinedresser'*. He goes on to explain to His listeners that His followers are branches of the vine, and that the only way they can produce fruit is to abide - stay connected to Jesus. That in fact, without staying attached to the main vine, they will not be able to produce anything of worth (v5).

Have you ever wondered why Jesus used the picture of a vine? Could he not have said that He was an olive tree, or a fig tree, perhaps? The picture would still have worked for any plant with fruit yielding branches. But His listeners would have understood why He called Himself the vine. In the Old Testament, the picture of vines and vineyards were often used to represent Israel. Most notably in Psalm 80:8-19 we have the description of a vine, brought out of Egypt, planted so that it took deep root and flourished. This is an obvious reference to God's chosen people. Yet the Psalm goes on to lament that God has let the hedges surrounding this vine / vineyard be broken down so that the fruit can be stolen, by thieves and wild beasts. The cry is for God to restore His vine and His vineyard.

Israel had been the people chosen by God to carry His presence and to declare His glory, but they had failed to do so through their sin and disobedience. So here in the New Testament Jesus stands up and says *'I am the Vine'*, and you all can be a part of Me. He was the restored vine that God had planted - and those who believed in Him would become God's chosen people to carry His presence and to reflect His glory. Not just those who listened to Jesus speak on that day, but the invitation to be grafted into that vine was for everyone, from that day on. Jew or gentile. All could become a part of God's new vine, by accepting Jesus as Lord and Saviour.

This new vine is designed to produce fruit that glorifies God. As branches of the vine we are not responsible for producing fruit in and of ourselves. Jesus is the one who produces His fruit from our submitted lives, as we stay connected to Him. It is evidenced in the way our character becomes more and more like His. It is the fruit of His spirit working in our lives (Galatians 5:22-23).

Sometimes He needs to prune things from our lives that prevent us bearing fruit. Sometimes He has to bind up the branches so that they can bear the weight of the fruit He wants us to produce. Always His Word brings the truth we need to keep our lives clean and attached to Him (John 15:1-7). Jesus, the Vine, asks us to abide in Him. To make Him our first focus and be willing to submit everything to Him. Then we will see His fruit flourish in our lives.

Ask Yourself: *What does abiding in Christ look like for me? Am I willing to spend time with Him and submit myself to His will in all things?*

Ask God: *Show me, Jesus, when I have tried to produce good fruit in and of myself, instead of focussing on abiding in You.*

Pray: *Thank You Jesus that all you ask me to do is to abide in You. Thank You that you do not expect me to work hard to try and produce the kind of fruit You require. Instead You promise to make my life fruitful if I keep closely connected to You. Thank you for all the evidences of the fruit of the Spirit in my life.*

Help me to stay connected to You even when things are difficult in my life. To be able to discern when You are doing a pruning work in me, and when You are asking me to trust You. Thank you for Your Word which shows me how to live connected to You, and highlights what things might threaten our connection. Help me to keep You as my first focus. I want to see fruit that glorifies God flourish in my life.

Amen.

Further Reading: John 15:1-17

DAY 6

LIGHT (OF THE WORLD)

"The people who sat in darkness have seen a great light,
And upon those who sat in the region and shadow of death
Light has dawned."
Matthew 4:16 NKJV

Matthew quotes these words from the prophet Isaiah (Isaiah 9:2) as he recorded the start of Jesus' earthly ministry. The gospel writer was declaring that Jesus was fulfilling that prophecy, that He was the Light that had come to transform the lives of those who walked in darkness and who lived in the shadow of death.

Simeon quoted another 'light' prophecy from the book of Isaiah (Isaiah 42:6) as he held the infant Christ in his arms in the Temple. He declared that Jesus, the Light, had come not just to His own people but as '*a light to bring revelation to the Gentiles*' (Luke 2:32).

A third prophetic reference to the Light that was to come can be found in Isaiah 60:1-3. Here the cry comes '*Arise Shine, for your Light has come!'*, with the promise that despite the encroaching darkness the Light will shine and that Gentiles (the nations) will be drawn to its brightness. Christ came, and with Him came Light.

The themes of darkness and light run throughout scripture. Darkness represents evil, sin, godlessness, fear, hopelessness, anxiety, despair, oppression, lack of sight, lack of wisdom or direction, and death. In contrast light signifies goodness, holiness, hope, joy, peace, vision, revelation, life and glory. Jesus came to turn darkness to light. John describes him as '*the light of men'*, a shining light that darkness could not understand or overcome (John 1:4-5). Jesus said of Himself *'I am the Light of the World, He that follows Me shall not walk in darkness but have the light of life'* (John 8:12). That's good news! There is no power of darkness that His light cannot dispel.

If we follow closely after Him, then all darkness must bow to His light. We can live in hope, joy, and revelation light, even when darkness is all around us. We can live in the light that He brings and turn our backs on the darkness that threatens. We can shine as He shines, showing His Light to a world trapped in darkness.

But it is a choice. Jesus warned His listeners in John 3:19-21 that darkness is powerful, and many still choose darkness over light. It is still a choice, even to those of us who already belong to Him. To be dragged back into walking/living in darkness, or to choose to stay close to Him and to walk in His light (1 John 1:5-7).

Jesus is the Light. In Him is goodness, holiness, hope, joy, peace, vision, revelation, life and glory.

Ask Yourself: *Am I shining Him? Do I bring light into dark situations? Do I carry hope, joy, goodness and peace?*

Ask God: *Show me, Jesus, the areas of my life where I have chosen not to walk in Your light.*

Pray: *Thank You Jesus that Your coming brought light into the darkness, and not just to the people who lived in the time that You walked on earth. Thank You that all peoples can be drawn towards Your light. All can choose to accept You and live in the Light that You brought. Thank You for the hope, joy, peace and life you bring.*

Thank You that however dark things might get, You are the Light that can dispel all darkness. Help me to choose to continue to walk in Your Light, so that I might shine as You shine and draw others to Your Light.

Amen.

Further Reading: John 1:1-13

REFLECTION

Which of the previous six descriptors of Jesus has impacted you most?

How has your heart and mind been illuminated afresh to see Jesus in a greater way than you have before?

What is the biggest personal challenge that you have taken from this section of devotionals?

As the busyness of the pre-Christmas season threatens to overwhelm and distract us from the real reason for our celebrations, it is good to remind ourselves that Jesus, Son of Man, is all that we need. He is our life-giving source of spiritual food and water, our solid foundation to build on, the only One who can produce lasting fruit in our lives, and the Light that dispels all darkness.

Thank you Jesus

PART II

PRINCE OF PEACE

AND HIS NAME SHALL BE CALLED...

Jesus is the promised Messiah,
The One promised for centuries before His birth.
The One who would come and establish a kingdom of peace,
By giving Himself in selfless sacrifice to make peace between ourselves and God.
The One who would inherit David's throne and who rules victorious.
Jesus, our Prince of Peace.

DAY 7

BRANCH

"Behold, the days are coming," says the LORD,
"That I will raise to David a Branch of righteousness;
A King shall reign and prosper,
And execute judgment and righteousness in the earth.
Jeremiah 23:5 NKJV

The little book of Zechariah gave us the prophecy describing Jesus as a fountain that we looked at on Day 2. Earlier in the book the prophet records another prophetic declaration, straight from the mouth of God, *'I am bringing forth My Servant the Branch'*, He says. (Zechariah 3:8)

If we look to the book of Jeremiah, we also see the Messiah referred to as branch. The One who is to come will be a *'Branch of righteousness'* and from the line of David, a King who will reign justly on the earth (Jeremiah 23:5). Isaiah also has a messianic prophecy about a 'branch', a *'Rod from the stem of Jesse'*, that *'shall grow out of his roots'* (Isaiah 11:1).

When we think of a branch we might picture the strong

branch of a gnarled old oak tree, but the meaning here is more like a sprout of fresh new growth that has the *potential* to become a strong branch. If a great tree like an oak is felled and a stump left, with its roots still in the ground, then it is quite possible for a new branch to begin to sprout and grow from it. The stump or stem in this case is the kingly line of David and his father Jesse, and the branch that will sprout from it will be a new and glorious king. This King would not be born in a palace of course, but in a Bethlehem stable.

The prophets were speaking at a time when the Kingdoms of Israel and Judah were disintegrating and suffering under a succession of evil and godless kings. The promise was for a King who would have a reign of righteousness; like David the great king that had once ruled a great Israel. But the reign of this promised King would even surpass that of David's.

The features of this King and His reign are described in Isaiah 11:1-10. Full of the Spirit and wisdom, fully submitted to God, and delighting in Him, the branch King will reign with righteousness, justice, faithfulness and compassion. His reign (Kingdom) will see the wolf lying down with the lamb, and the earth full of the knowledge of God. Gentiles (the nations) will seek Him and His kingdom.

This is our Jesus, the King whose reign has begun but will come into its fullness in eternity, when the heavens and earth are made new, and sin and death, evil and darkness will no longer have any power.

Ask Yourself: *Is my life well rooted in God and in His promises, so that even when things seem to be cut off, or come to an end, God can still cause something new to grow from me?*

Ask God: *Show me, Jesus, where I have not trusted You, or what You have promised, especially when the wait has been long to see the promises fulfilled.*

Pray: *Thank You Jesus that You came as God's fulfilled promise, not only to His people, but to all of mankind. Thank You that You are the perfect righteous, rightful King, and that You will bring Your Kingdom rule into reality here on earth as it is in heaven. Thank You that You reign with righteousness, faithfulness, compassion and justice.*

Help me to acknowledge You as King in every part of my life, and to do all that I can, in partnership with You, to see your Kingdom come into its full fulfilment, here on earth.

Amen.

Further Reading: Psalm 72

DAY 8

SERVANT

"Behold! My Servant whom I uphold,
My Elect One in whom My soul delights!
I have put My Spirit upon Him;
He will bring forth justice to the Gentiles."
Isaiah 42:1 NKJV

Within the book of Isaiah there are very many prophetic references to the coming Messiah. They encompass many different names and ways of describing the Saviour. In Isaiah 42:1, God declares the one to come as, '*My Servant*'. He is going to be a Servant that God has chosen, that God delights in, that will bring restoration to Israel, and be a light to the nations. Isaiah 49:6 tells us that this Servant will bring '*salvation to the ends of the earth.*'

Back in Isaiah 42:1-4, we learn more about this Servant. He will carry the Spirit of God and will bring justice - a form of justice that doesn't crush the already bruised. Matthew quotes Isaiah's prophetic words in Matthew 12:18-21. Jesus is ministering to the multitudes, and healing many. He is full of God's Spirit and serving humanity, with compassion and gentleness. We know that Isaiah's prophecy about a Servant is talking about Jesus because Matthew confirms it for us.

In the New Testament, in Philippians 2:, Paul talks about Jesus as the one who *'made Himself of no reputation, taking the form of a bondservant'*. A bondservant is one who knows they have no rights of their own and has to submit themselves to obey and serve the one in authority over them. Jesus willingly left behind any rights He had as God's Son and took the form of a servant, demonstrating this in the washing of the disciples' feet in John 13. He came willingly submitted to God's authority and lovingly enslaved to Him, obedient all the way to death on the cross. It was His choice to make Himself as a servant, and God honoured Him for it *'My elect one in whom my soul delights'* (Isaiah 42:1).

Jesus came as a servant in order to bring about our salvation, and in doing so Jesus gave us the supreme example of servanthood. But did coming as a servant lessen His power, authority or kingship? No! That is the most amazing thing. He came as a servant, but also as a king. He showed us that true leadership requires humility, compassion and a servant heart - towards those we are called to serve, and towards the One who calls us.

The Servant King shows us that we are called to be lovingly enslaved to God, and lovingly enslaved to one another.

Ask Yourself: *What does it look like for me to be lovingly enslaved to God? How can I serve Him by serving others?*

Ask God: *Show me, Jesus, how much You delight in me. Remind me that You are worth serving because of how much You love me.*

Pray: *Thank You Jesus that You chose to come to earth as a man and took the form of a Servant. Thank You for being willing to serve Your Father and to serve mankind. Thank You that You served out of love and compassion, with justice and gentleness. Thank You for giving us the supreme example of what it looks like to serve God and our fellow man.*

Help me to remember that to have a servant heart is not a weak thing. It is empowering and God honouring. True leaders know how to serve well. You showed us the way. Thank you Jesus.

Amen.

Further Reading: John 13:1-17

DAY 9

LAMB OF GOD

"Behold! The Lamb of God who takes away the sin of the world!"
John 1:29

John the Baptist was baptising in the Jordan when he saw Jesus approaching. *'Behold! The Lamb of God, who takes away the sin of the world!'* he declared (John 1:29). The next day he declared the same, and two of his disciples immediately left him to follow Jesus (John 1:35-36). John could have said, 'behold the Messiah', or 'behold the Son of God', but he didn't. We can't know for sure, but I wonder if those two disciples understood the name that John the Baptist gave Jesus? It seems it was enough for them to leave John and follow after Him.

It was likely they did understand, in part at least, as for them 'lamb' would have signified sacrifice. They had grown up under a Covenant where lambs were routinely offered as sacrifices for the atonement of sin, as laid down in Levitical law. John was describing Jesus as just such a sacrifice, and in this case, not for the sin of an individual, or even for a nation, but for the sin of the whole world.

Only lambs without blemish were considered fit to be offered as sacrifices in the Temple. And in his first epistle that is how Peter describes Jesus. As the One who shed His blood for our redemption, *'as of a lamb without blemish and without spot'* (1 Peter 1:18-19). Before even the laws of sacrifices were established, God had told His people to take and kill a lamb without blemish, and paint its blood on the doorposts of their homes, to protect themselves from the Angel of Death, at the first Passover (Exodus 12:3-7, 13). The blood of the lamb was their protection and their salvation.

Jesus was spotless. He *'knew no sin'* (2 Corinthians 5:21) and so could offer up Himself as the perfect sacrifice to make atonement for our sins. His blood was spilt, and stained the uprights and crossbeam of a wooden cross, so that the punishment of death would pass over us.

We don't see the description of Jesus as Lamb of God anywhere else in the Gospels, but it is an eternal theme. In Heaven that is how Jesus appears - as a Lamb that had been slain (Revelation 5:6), and it is as the Lamb of God that He is eternally worshipped.

'Worthy is the Lamb who was slain, to receive power and riches and wisdom, and strength and honour, and glory and blessing!'
Revelation 5:12

We are undeserving of His great sacrifice. We could not atone for our own sin, and even the sacrifice of animals could not fully wipe the slate clean. But God provided the Lamb, the spotless Lamb without blemish, and He, Himself, gave His life willingly, so that our sin and guilt is atoned for. Eternally.

***Ask Yourself**: Am I as quick to leave everything and follow the Lamb of God, as John's disciples were?*

***Ask God**: Show me, Jesus, what thing I need to bring to the foot of Your cross. Sins that Your death has atoned for but that I need to repent of.*

***Pray:** Thank You Jesus, Lamb of God, that You lived a blameless life and gave Your life willingly as an atoning sacrifice for my sin. Thank You that is was Your great love for me that drove You to offer Yourself, dying so that I could live. Thank You that Your death was the once and for all sacrifice that redeems me to live forever free from the power of sin and death.*

Help me to follow close after You, Jesus, and by the help of Your spirit, to live a life that is holy and acceptable to You. When I am tempted to sin, help me to remember what it cost You to purchase my redemption. You are the exalted Lamb of God, seated at the right hand of the Father in heaven, and You deserve all my praise, worship and adoration, today and forever.

Amen.

***Further Reading**:* Hebrews 10:11-25

DAY 10

REDEEMER

'For I know that my Redeemer lives, And He shall stand at last on the earth'
Job 19:25 NKJV

In Isaiah 59:20, God declares *'The Redeemer will come to Zion'*. Many times, in the Old Testament, God refers to Himself as the Redeemer, but in this instance, He is talking of the One to come. We know this as this verse is quoted in Romans 11:26 and most definitely refers to Jesus, although the New Testament writer uses 'deliverer' instead of 'redeemer'.

When His parents came to the Temple to present the infant Jesus to the Lord, they were met by Anna, a widow who had worshipped in the Temple for many years, praying and waiting for the Messiah to appear. Anna recognised Jesus for who He was, and could not help but tell all of those, who like herself had *'looked for redemption in Jerusalem'*. She knew that her Redeemer had come. (Luke 2:36-38)

So, what does 'redeemer' mean? If you look up the word

'redeem' in the dictionary you can find several meanings for the word. We can talk about redeeming our reputation, if we have behaved badly, by doing a good deed. Or we can redeem an unpleasant thing or situation by seeing some good in it, finding its 'redeeming feature'. But the definitions that involve payment of some kind are what we are talking about here. You can redeem a debt by paying back what is owed, or you can redeem an object that once belonged to you, regaining possession of it by paying a price. It means to buy something back.

This is what God did through Christ. We were made for God, made to be the object of His love and to share in close intimate relationship with Him. Our sin and disobedience separated us from God; in a sense we were lost to Him. He had to pay to get us back. And we owed a debt to Him that we could never pay, but He took care of it all. And with what a payment! 1 Peter 1:18-19 tell us that it wasn't with *'silver or gold'*, that are undoubtedly precious but will still corrupt over time, but *'with the precious blood of Christ'* that He redeemed us. Our redemption cost Jesus His life.

In fact, in the Hebrew, the term 'redeemer' implies something more than just buying back; it suggests the requirement that it be person of close relationship that does the redeeming. This is beautifully illustrated in the story of Ruth and Boaz (Ruth 4). The 'kinsman redeemer' had a responsibility to take under his care and protection one who was vulnerable through widowhood or abandonment. This wasn't the act of a stranger, but someone closely related.

Jesus chose to redeem us, not as a stranger, but as one who already loved us unconditionally. He took on the role of our kinsman redeemer so that we can come under His care and protection. Not only are we bought back by Him, but we are brought into His family, to be loved and secure for all eternity.

Ask Yourself: *How does seeing Jesus as my kinsman redeemer help me to understand how much He truly cares for me? Is it hard for me to accept that He loves me unconditionally?*

Ask God: *Show me, Jesus, any areas of my life where I have been unwilling to submit to Your care and protection.*

Pray: *Thank You Jesus, for being my redeemer. Thank You for paying the debt that I could not, for giving Yourself to buy me back, and for what it cost You. Thank you Father that You loved me enough to want me back in close relationship with You. Thank you Jesus, that as You are my kinsman redeemer, I can be secure in Your love and protection for all eternity.*

Help me God to truly understand how much You love me and want to be close to me. Help me to be quick to tell those who need to hear it, that redemption has come in the form of Your Son. And that the price He paid was to redeem all who are willing to believe in Him, and come back to Him in repentance. Thank You for my redemption.

Amen.

Further Reading: Ephesians 1:3-12

DAY 11

BRIDEGROOM

And Jesus said, "Can the friends of the bridegroom mourn as long as the bridegroom is with them? But the days will come when the bridegroom will be taken away from them, and then they will fast."
Matthew 9:15 NKJV

One of the most beautiful descriptions of Jesus is that of the bridegroom. There are two places in the gospels where this description is used. In John 3:28-30 John the Baptist refers to Jesus as the bridegroom. Reports have been brought to him by his disgruntled disciples that Jesus is baptising and drawing a huge crowd. To re-iterate what he has already told them he says these words, *'You yourselves bear me witness, that I said, 'I am not the Christ,' but, 'I have been sent before Him.' He who has the bride is the bridegroom; but the friend of the bridegroom, who stands and hears him, rejoices greatly because of the bridegroom's voice. Therefore this joy of mine is fulfilled.'* John is exalting Christ as the bridegroom and is joy-filled to be His friend, the one sent to prepare the way and to wait for Him to come.

Jesus also described Himself as the bridegroom. Again it is John the Baptist's disciples who are seeking clarification. They are questioning Jesus as to why His disciples were not fasting, as they and the Pharisees did. Jesus' response is to compare Himself to a bridegroom throwing a party (Matthew 9:15). Why should they be miserable when the time they have left with the bridegroom was time for celebration? He would be leaving them soon enough.

The bridegroom theme was one that Jesus' listeners would have been familiar with; God Himself described Himself as the bridegroom, *And as the bridegroom rejoices over the bride, So shall your God rejoice over you* (Isaiah 62:5).

In Hebrew tradition the bride would get herself prepared on her wedding day, and sit beautifully dressed waiting patiently at her family home until her bridegroom and his friends came calling. Her bridegroom would then come and take her back with him to his own home. What a wonderful picture for us. Jesus, our bridegroom, is coming for us. We are waiting for that day when He comes to take us home with Him.

Do you feel you are not worthy to be His bride? Revelation 21:2 assures us that the bride (the church) that Jesus is coming for is already beautifully adorned, dressed ready for her bridegroom, because He has already made us pure and spotless (Ephesians 5:25-27).

And how does Jesus feel about us His bride? Well just turn to Song of Solomon, which is a beautiful love song between the bridegroom and His bride, and a glorious picture of Christ wooing us. Song of Solomon 4:9 says *'you have ravished my heart, My sister, My spouse'*. He is completely besotted with us. He is the lover of our souls. Transfixed by our beauty, He can't wait for the day when He comes and makes us fully His for all eternity.

***Ask Yourself**: Do I struggle to relate to Jesus as bridegroom? Why is that?*

***Ask God**: Show me, Jesus, how much You delight in me and how beautiful I am to You.*

***Pray:** Thank You Jesus that You are the perfect bridegroom. Thank You that You loved me and gave Yourself for me, so that I could be Your bride. Thank You that You clothe me with Your righteousness so that I am worthy to be Your spotless bride. Thank You that You are coming back to claim me as Your own.*

Jesus, help me to understand that You see me as beautiful and lovely. That You love being my bridegroom and chose me for Yourself. Help me to be ready for Your return; I long to be with You forever.

Amen.

Further Reading: Song of Solomon 2:8-14

DAY 12

RULER

"But you, Bethlehem Ephrathah,
Though you are little among the thousands of Judah,
Yet out of you shall come forth to Me
The One to be Ruler in Israel"
Micah 5:2

We read in Matthew 2 of the Magi coming to Jerusalem looking for the promised King of the Jews, having seen a sign in the heavens. They came to Jerusalem and to King Herod because they were expecting a prince born in a palace. But we know that this King was to be born in much more humble circumstances. The scholars of Herod's court knew where to send the Magi, because of the prophecy in Micah 5:2 – that out of Bethlehem would come *'The One to be Ruler in Israel'*.

Many of our favourite fairy tales and fictional stories explore the theme of a good ruler coming whose power and authority would turn bad to good and restore society to what it should be: Robin Hood, The Chronicles of Narnia, The Lord of the Rings. Israel was waiting for their promised King, but they were also waiting for His righteous reign. They were living under oppression and injustice and they believed that this new king would make all things right for them.

There was so much expectation. Those who were waiting for this new King of the Jews believed He would be a ruler to crush Roman cruelty and to restore peace and prosperity to Israel. But Jesus was going to be a different kind of ruler; a ruler of hearts and minds. His reign would be a spiritual one bringing the realities of the Kingdom of Heaven to earth.

Jesus does restore, He does turn bad to good; He makes all things new (Revelation 21:5). But He requires us to acknowledge Him as King. It is His right, and one day He will reign over all creation, *'the government will be upon His shoulder'* (Isaiah 9:6). Our response must be to submit to Him as ruler of our hearts and lives. Then He can bring about transformational change in us. For the good.

The Magi found their way to Bethlehem, and the child they encountered there was a King. A King that would turn the world upside down; by His life and death He would prove Himself ruler of all. The *'Lion of the tribe of Judah'*, the one who carries the sceptre and who wears the crown (Revelation 5:5, Genesis 49:10), stands in heaven as the One worthy of all our praise and adoration. Forever.

Ask Yourself: *Am I always willing to let Jesus be the Ruler of my heart, and especially of my mind?*

Ask God: *Show me, Jesus, when I have expected you to do something that wasn't in Your plan to do, and if I have missed what You were really doing.*

Pray: *Thank You Jesus that You are king. I cannot ask for a more perfect Ruler. Thank You that You came to transform the world and to transform me. Thank You that You want to reign in my life, and that I can trust You to do that in the way that is best for me. Thank You that one day You will make all things new and that You will reign over Your Kingdom forever.*

Help me to submit my heart and mind to your perfect rule. Help me to give You the place of rulership in my life, today and every day. You deserve that place, and I honour You as my King, just as all of heaven worships You.

Amen.

Further Reading: Revelation 5

REFLECTION

Which of the previous six descriptors of Jesus has impacted you most?

How has your heart and mind been illuminated afresh to see Jesus in a greater way than you have before?

What is the biggest personal challenge that you have taken from this section of devotionals?

Wise Men from the East followed a star because of a promise of a longed-for King. That King came, not to a palace, but to a stable, and then to the hearts of men. Jesus showed us through His perfect obedience to the Father, through His willingness to lay down His life, what true servant-hearted leadership looks like. He is our Redeemer and our Bridegroom, He loves us deeply and we can trust Him. With every area of our lives. He is our perfect Ruler and one day will reign over all creation. Our perfect Prince of Peace.

Thank you Jesus

PART III

MIGHTY GOD, EVERLASTING FATHER

AND HIS NAME SHALL BE CALLED...

Jesus is God Incarnate.
The One who came to reveal the Father to us,
Who would show us the Father's heart in shepherding and protecting us.
He was at creation, He spoke the Word and it was done.
He is the Word of God.
He is Truth.
He is the great I AM.
Mighty God, Everlasting Father.

DAY 13

SHEPHERD

'I am the good shepherd. The good shepherd gives His life for the sheep'
John 10:11

Psalm 23 is perhaps the most familiar and most quoted of all the Psalms. David the Psalmist describes the Lord as his shepherd, the one who leads, feeds and protects him. The theme is explored with even more depth in Ezekiel 34, where God describes Himself as the true shepherd to His people. In verse 23 of that chapter He talks of the *'one shepherd'* to come, calling Him his *'servant David'*. Now as Ezekiel was prophesying long after the death of King David this can only refer to Jesus, David's greater son.

So is God the shepherd of His people, or is Jesus? Well both are of course! Because Jesus came from the Father and He and the Father are one (John 10:30).

One of the most beautiful descriptions of *how* He shepherds is in Isaiah 40:11,

He will feed His flock like a shepherd;
He will gather the lambs with His arm,
And carry them in His bosom,
And gently lead those who are with young.

This is the Father's heart towards us.

In John 10:11-16 Jesus describes Himself as the '*good shepherd*', as the one who would give His life for His sheep, and as the one who intimately knows His own.

'*I am the good shepherd; and I know My sheep, and am known by My own*' (v14).

When Jesus came, Israel was a people without a true shepherd, '*weary and scattered*' (Matthew 9:36). Sheep without a shepherd are vulnerable in every sense. A good shepherd in Jesus' time was much more than just a leader or guide, he was one who cared deeply for the sheep in his care, would ensure they were fed, rested, and safe at all times. He would give his very life to protect them and cared that not even one sheep went astray.

Jesus came to offer Himself to the people of Israel as the true shepherd His Father had promised them, and for those who accepted Him that is what He became. He offers the same for us. When we belong to Him, we are the sheep of His pasture and He is the Shepherd of our souls (1 Peter 2:25). Jesus seeks out and brings the wandering ones back to Himself. In His fold we can live secure. We can trust Him - to guide us, feed us, care for us and protect us. Even to carry us close to His heart when that is what we need.

Ask Yourself: *Do I ever find my heart wandering from Him? Have I practised listening for His voice so that I can hear Him call me back when I do wander?*

Ask God: *Show me, Jesus, when I have tried to be self-sufficient. I give you permission to carry me, submitting myself into your safe arms.*

Pray: *Thank You Jesus that You are my good shepherd. You are the perfect shepherd, who knows me intimately. You know what I need and how to meet those needs. You lead me where I need to go, feed me and give me rest in You. Your kind shepherd's heart reveals the Father's heart towards me.*

Help me to trust You, particularly when I don't understand where You are leading, or when things get tough. You are still my good shepherd in those tough times, and I place myself into Your arms, asking You to carry me close to Your heart.

Amen.

Further Reading: Ezekiel 34:11-31

DAY 14

THE DOOR

'I am the door.
If anyone enters by Me, he will be saved, and will go in and out and find pasture.'
John 10:9

In the same chapter of John's Gospel where Jesus describes Himself as the good shepherd, He also describes Himself as the *door*, or *gate*, to the sheep (John 10:7). This would have conjured up a wonderful picture for those listening to Him. Sheepfolds of the time were roofless, and constructed of stone walls with a gap left for the sheep to enter and exit. This gap would have no physical gate. Once all the sheep were safely herded in, then the shepherds would take turns to sit in the gap. They would protect the sheep with their own bodies, keeping them in peace and safety, and only letting other shepherds who they knew near the sheep. They were a physical barrier against thieves and wild animals. So the door and the shepherd were one and the same thing.

. . .

The Greek word for door used in John 10:7 and again in v9 can also be translated as 'entrance, passage, or way'. In calling Himself the door, Jesus was re-emphasising the truth that He had come to be the *only way* to the Father. Jesus says *'I am THE WAY, the truth and the Life. No-one comes to the Father except by Me'* (John 14:6).

In John 10:9 He states that those who 'enter' through Him, will be saved. They will become sheep of His sheepfold. Free to go in and out, following Him to the best pastures, and following Him to the best places to rest. In John 10:10 He makes this promise concerning His 'sheep', *'I have come that they may have life, and that they may have it more abundantly'.*

There is a warning though. The doorway is a narrow one and not always easy to enter (Luke 13:24). It might be off-putting to some. Believing in Jesus demands we lay down everything else at His feet. Yes, the life He promises is one of abundance, a life that will last for eternity. But it might cost. It may not be easy to follow the Shepherd.

How beautiful a shepherd He is that He laid down His life to be the doorway to the fold that is His kingdom!

How wonderful that we know we are secure in Him, and that although following Him might not always be easy, He will always protect and guard us. And His gift to us is life in abundance.

Ask Yourself*: Do I ever doubt His ability to protect me? Especially when life does not feel abundant?*

Ask God: *Show me, Jesus, the times where I have stepped outside of Your protection by trying to do things my own way.*

Pray: *Thank You Jesus that You are the Door. You, Yourself are both the Shepherd and the Gateway to the fold. Thank you that you laid down Your life to be the way for me to come back into relationship with the Father. Thank you that You protect me, even when I don't appreciate it. Thank You for all the times that you have prevented the 'thieves' and 'wild animals' from stealing from me. Show me how abundant my life is in You.*

Help me, Jesus to trust You to protect me at all times. Thank You that I am a sheep of Your fold, and that is the very best, safest, most life-giving place to be. I am safe in Your fold for all eternity. I bring to You now those whom I love who have yet to find You, the door, and pray that they too will enter in to find abundant, eternal life in You.

Amen.

Further Reading: John 10:1-30

DAY 15

SUN OF RIGHTEOUSNESS

"But to you who fear My name
The Sun of Righteousness shall arise
With healing in His wings;"
Malachi 4:2

There are lines in the carol 'Hark the Herald Angels Sing', that you've probably sung many, many times: 'Hail the Son of Righteousness, Life and Light to all He brings, Risen with healing in His wings'.

The scripture it comes from is Malachi 4:2, and it is not actually the 'son' but the 'sun' of righteousness. This makes more sense when you realise that 'wings' can also be translated as 'rays'. The picture Malachi gives us is of a bright shining sun, whose rays are full of healing life.

Sunlight is necessary for all life and growth. As the sun rises in the morning it brings light and warmth. In the same way, Jesus the sun comes, and His rising brings light that dispels darkness, and brings warmth and healing. He brings life itself to all who will fall under His rays.

In 2 Samuel 23:4, David speaks of a just ruler to come, in beautiful poetic language,

'And he shall be like the light of the morning when the sun rises,

A morning without clouds,

Like the tender grass springing out of the earth, By clear shining after rain.'

This is the Sun of Righteousness.

We saw earlier that God promised a *'Branch of righteousness'* to come, in Jeremiah 23:5. In the very next verse He uses the same word translated as 'righteousness' again in giving this branch, this King, the title *'the Lord Our Righteousness'* or *Jehovah Tsidkenu* (Jeremiah 23:6). He is altogether right, just and holy.

This Sun is He whose face *'was like the sun shining in its strength'* in John's vision (Revelation 1:16). His coming was the dawn, the *'Dayspring'* (Luke 1:78) that a jubilant Zachariah (the Father of John the Baptist) sang of. The one who came to dispel the darkness of sin and death and to bring a glorious righteous brightness. Just like the rising sun brings hope for a new day, just like the sun feeds the earth with its warmth, causing life and healing, so in His holy sunshine rays are our life and healing.

So now when you sing 'Hark the Herald angels sing' and get to those lines you can sing with a deeper understanding of what they mean. And you can change the 'Son' to 'Sun', no one will notice!

Ask Yourself: *Do I choose to live in the hope that His rising brings? Or do I let my life circumstances keep me dark places?*

Ask God: *Show me, Jesus, how your righteous light can bring healing into my life by illuminating the things that need to be dealt with.*

Pray: *Thank You Jesus, that You are my Sun of Righteousness. Living in your light can bring hope and healing. Thank you that like the dawn, You bring me new hope every day. Help me to choose to live in the hope that You offer even in the dark times. Thank you that Your face shines towards me and that I live in the glorious brightness of Your favour.*

Help me to live aware of Your warmth and light. You are my righteousness and I want to live a life that pleases you. Make me holy as You are holy.

Amen.

Further Reading: Luke 1:67-79

DAY 16

TRUTH

'I am the way, the TRUTH and the life.'
John 14:6

Jesus said in John 14:6, *'I am the way, the TRUTH and the life'*. He said He was 'the way', and 'the life' in response to Thomas' inquiry as to how they could follow Him where He was going. But what did He mean when He said He was 'the truth'?

When Jesus stood before Pilate, He declared Himself to be the One bearing *'witness to the truth'*, and that the only those *'of the truth'* would hear His voice (John 18:37-38). Pilate's reply echoes through history, the cry of a searching humanity; *'What is truth*?' The irony for Pilate was that truth was standing right before Him in the person of Jesus.

The word 'truth' here isn't just simply the opposite of a lie. It means much more. In fact, it was used in Greek to describe the opposite of 'illusion'. 'Truth' meant reality. Truth meant all things genuine, the embodiment of moral truth and rightness, the proof of what was true. So when Jesus declared that He was truth, He was in effect saying, 'I am reality, and much of what this world offers is merely illusion. I am the real thing, genuine, right, certain, the only truth worthy of your complete trust'.

Knowing the truth isn't just about gaining enough head knowledge to persuade ourselves to believe. Knowing the truth is knowing and trusting Jesus. John 8:32, says, '*you shall know the truth and the truth shall make you free*'. The context of this is abiding in the Word of God, but it applies equally to the One who declared 'I am truth'.

We trust those who are truthful and operate with integrity, but even those we are closest to will sometimes let us down. It is difficult to always be completely truthful and genuine, because we are flawed human beings. But there is one who is perfectly true and genuine, and He can be completely trusted. He is the answer to the world's search for truth and reality. He is the victorious, gloriously risen Jesus, that John saw riding on a white horse, whose name is '*FAITHFUL AND TRUE*' (Revelation 19:11).

Ask Yourself: *Have I sought for the truth by trying to gain head knowledge, rather than abiding in the One who calls Himself 'the truth', and in what He says?*

Ask God: *Show me, Jesus, where I have looked to other things as 'reality' when in fact they are an illusion compared to You.*

Pray: *Thank You Jesus, that You are Truth. You are the only true reality. You and the message You bring are genuine and true. The way You love me is real and You can be trusted. Believing in You as truth has the power to set me free. And You are this world's only hope as they seek for truth.*

Jesus, help me to always strive to live with truth and integrity in my life, so that I reflect who You are. Help me to trust that what You say, and who You are, is true. Forgive me when I have pursued head knowledge, or looked to the things of this world, in my own search for what truth is. Help me to point others to the truth, to point them to You. Thank You Jesus.

Amen.

Further Reading: Ephesians 4:17-24

DAY 17

WORD

And the Word became flesh and dwelt among us,
and we beheld His glory, the glory as of the only begotten of the Father,
full of grace and truth.
John 1:14

John's gospel begins with the familiar words, '*In the beginning was the Word, and the Word was with God, and the Word was God* ' (John 1:1). To know he is speaking of Jesus we only have to jump down to v14, and to these words, '*And the Word became flesh and dwelt among us, and we beheld His glory, the glory as of the only begotten of the Father, full of grace and truth.*'

I wonder if you have ever struggled to understand this description of Jesus? I certainly have. I love words, I love reading them and writing them. I love the beauty words can portray when used creatively. So how does this relate to Jesus? The Greek meaning of 'word' here isn't so much the written word but the spoken word, or '*logos*'. It is the expression of a thought. It makes much more sense to describe Jesus in this way, as the spoken, outward expression of God's thoughts. The manifestation of all that He is.

Scripture tells us that *'out of the abundance of the heart the mouth speaks'* (Matthew 12:34). God had so much in His heart that He wanted to express to mankind of His love, joy, truth, holiness, grace and mercy, that He sent us His spoken message in the person of Christ. In effect Jesus was the embodiment of all that God wanted to say to us. How beautiful is that!

But there is more. John 1:1-3 tell us that Jesus was there in eternity with God and through Him all creation happened (Colossians 1:16). We know that God spoke creation into being (Genesis 1:3). It was in His heart already, but speaking the words had the power to bring what was in His heart to life. In and through Jesus, God speaks the desire of His heart, to bring life, eternal life, life in abundance to all who will believe.

Jesus is *'the Word of life'* (1 John 1:1). In Revelation John describes Jesus as the all victorious One riding on a white horse, bearing the words *'faithful and true'*. He gives Him the name *'The Word of God'* (Revelation 19:11-13). This is the One who shed His blood and rose again to purchase life for us. He wears the victor's crown.

As John declares, of Jesus, the Word,

In Him was life, and the life was the light of men (John 1:4).

Ask Yourself: *How does seeing Jesus as God, the One who created the world, and who is the human expression of God in all His fullness, change the way I understand the nature of God?*

Ask God: *Show me, Jesus, how powerful my words are. They have the power to bring life or to bring death (Proverbs 18:21).*

Pray: *Thank You Jesus, that You are the living Word. You are the full expression of God and You came to earth to show us the Father. Thank You that as God's Word you offer life to all who will accept You. You are the Word of Life.*

Help me to see You as God, to acknowledge You as the creator of the world, and to worship You as the victorious One. Help me to understand that just as Your words have power to create, and to express God's heart, so do mine. Help me to speak of God's love and mercy with my words, but also with my life, as You did.

Amen.

Further Reading: John 1:1-18

DAY 18

I AM

Jesus said to them, "Most assuredly, I say to you, before Abraham was, I AM."
John 8:58

In John 8:58, Jesus said something extraordinary which astounded His listeners, *'before Abraham was, I Am'*. He was claiming to have existed before Abraham lived on earth. The Jewish leaders and scholars could make no sense of that, how the man who stood before them could claim to have also been alive before the man who was the great father of their nation. Unless… He was claiming to be more than a man.

His wording was no mistake. He did not say the more grammatically correct, 'before Abraham was, I was'. He said 'I AM'. In fact He had already used the phrase 'I am' twice in this discourse, in John 8:24, and again in John 8:28 (it is written as *'I am He'* but the *'He'* is not there in the Greek). If they hadn't got it before, I believe they would have heard it for sure the third time. And it angered them so much they wanted to kill Jesus on the spot. Because His listeners would have known those two words as the title God used of Himself when He talked to Moses from the burning bush, *'I AM WHO I AM'* (Exodus 3:14). That is, I am the One that just exists, the One that is, and always has been, and always will be. The eternal One who is all, and holds all in His hands.

Jesus was claiming deity. He did it again in John 18:5-6, when the soldiers came to arrest Him in the garden of Gethsemane. And either consciously or sub-consciously, they knew the power in His words. When they told Him they had come seeking Jesus of Nazareth, He said, *'I am'* (again, the *'He'* is not there in the Greek). At His words the soldiers fell back to the ground. And so God, in human form, allowed Himself to be taken by cruel human hands and led to His death, for our salvation.

Be in no doubt, the baby that shepherds ran to find, and that kings knelt to worship, was and is the great I AM. The same God of the burning bush, who delivered His people from Egypt and parted the Red Sea, came in the form of a baby to Bethlehem. God the Son was not a lesser version of God the Father, or just a part of Him. He was, and is, God eternal.

'I am the Alpha and the Omega, the Beginning and the End', He declares from heaven (Revelation 1:8). This is the One who deserves all our honour, all our praise, and our very lives in worship this Christmas. So, so much more than a baby in a manger.

Ask Yourself: *Do I ever lose the truth and wonder of who Jesus truly is, in celebrating the birth of a baby in Bethlehem?*

Ask God: *Show me, Jesus, what it means to me personally that you are my I AM. The One who is all, and holds all in His hands.*

Pray: *Thank You Jesus, that you are the great I AM. Thank You that You were, You are, and You always will be exactly all that You say You are. You exist outside of our time and of our understanding, and yet You humbled Yourself to live among us. You slept in the arms of a young woman, and You allowed Yourself to be taken by human hands and subjected to a cruel death. And yet You were and are God.*

Thank You that just as You delivered Your people Israel from slavery in Egypt, so You have delivered me from slavery to sin. You were all that they needed, their I AM. And you are all that I need, my I AM. Help me, especially as I celebrate Your birth this Christmas, to recognise and worship You as the I AM, and not just as a child in a manger.

Amen

Further Reading: John 8:13-30

REFLECTION

Which of the previous six descriptors of Jesus has impacted you most?

How has your heart and mind been illuminated afresh to see Jesus in a greater way than you have before?

What is the biggest personal challenge that you have taken from this section of devotionals?

The child born in a stable, and the man who stood before those who rejected and accused Him, was more than just a human being. Jesus was God's expression. Jesus was Truth, Light and Life. The only Way to be reconciled to the Father. The great Shepherd who loved His sheep enough to lay down His life for them. This Jesus, the great I AM, is our mighty God and our Everlasting Father.

Thank you Jesus

PART IV

FOR UNTO US A CHILD IS BORN, UNTO US A SON IS GIVEN

Jesus is God's Beloved Son, the One the Father delights in,
The long promised Son of David.
Born as a baby into poverty and obscurity,
But born as a glorious King.
Born to live among us,
To live within us,
God With Us.
Our comfort and our battle cry,
JESUS OUR SAVIOUR

DAY 19

BELOVED SON

And suddenly a voice came from heaven, saying,
"This is My beloved Son, in whom I am well pleased."
Matthew 3:17

The Angel Gabriel came to Mary and declared that the child she would conceive by the Holy Spirit would be called the *'Son of the Highest'* (Luke 1:32). On two further occasions God Himself speaks confirming Jesus as His Son: at His Baptism (Matthew 3:17), and at the Transfiguration (Matthew 17:5). On both occasions God declares *'This is my Beloved Son, in whom I am well pleased'*.

Can you picture God the Father, looking down with His heart bursting with love and pride for His Son? Those of us who are parents can perhaps understand that feeling. I know that we can't wait to tell people how wonderful our children, or our grandchildren are, and how proud we are of them. We see beyond their mistakes and imperfections and love them fiercely and unconditionally. Seeing God as a loving parent dispels the idea of Him being a distant figure. He was completely and utterly besotted with His son, His perfect Son, and was totally invested in what Jesus was doing. Isaiah 42:1 tells us that Jesus, His servant, delights God's soul.

But not only did God the Father love His Son, He loved the world that He sent His Son to (John 3:16). So much so that He willingly gifted His only son to the world. Jesus, the Son, came, sharing the very nature of His Father. He became the expression of the Father's love for us: love incarnate, willing to lay down His very life for us.

As parents we love to give our children what they wish for, especially at Christmas. If we could afford it, we would give our children the world. Funnily enough that was exactly what God the Father promised His Son,

'You are My Son,
Today I have begotten You.
Ask of Me, and I will give You
The nations for Your inheritance,
And the ends of the earth for Your possession.'
Psalm 2:7-8

That inheritance includes you and me! Because Jesus came willingly and obediently to earth, and humbled Himself to death on the cross, God exalted His Beloved Son to the highest place. And every knee in heaven and earth will one day bow to His beautiful name (Philippians 2:8-11).

***Ask Yourself**: Do I find it hard to see God as a loving father? Why is that?*

***Ask God**: Reveal to my heart, Jesus, just how much you love me personally.*

***Pray:** Thank You Father that You loved the world enough to send Your Beloved Son to live among us, and to die for us. Thank You that just as You delighted in Jesus, so You delight in me as Your child. Even when I make mistakes, it doesn't change how You love me, and You demonstrated that love for me in sending Jesus. Thank You that I am part of Jesus' inheritance, and that one day I will worship at His feet, knowing that I belong to Him.*

Help me to see how much You love and delight in me. Help me to love Jesus as He deserves to be loved, and to walk in His love.

Amen

Further Reading: Luke 1:26-38

DAY 20

IMMANUEL

"Behold, the virgin shall be with child, and bear a Son, and they shall call His name Immanuel," which is translated, "God with us."

Matthew 1:23

In Matthew 1:18 -21 we are told the story of Joseph, and his dream encounter with an angel of the Lord. Joseph is told that He should not be afraid to take Mary as his wife, as the child she carries was conceived by the Holy Spirit. Then in the following verses Matthew adds a quote from Isaiah (Matthew 1:22-23). Jesus' birth is going to fulfil another messianic prophecy. He will be called *'Immanuel'* which means *'God with us'* (Isaiah 7:14). It wasn't to be His actual name, rather an expression of what His coming meant.

God Himself, in the person of His Son, descended into humanity so that He could live among us. We can put from our minds all thoughts of a distant, uninterested God. Jesus was born into poverty, hardship, shame, fear and uncertainty, under Roman oppression. He chose to experience these things, as well as injustice, hatred, misunderstanding, loneliness, physical torture and death. Jesus suffered these willingly, for our salvation, but also so that He could fully understand our pain and suffering (Hebrews 4:15).

He truly made Himself God with man, and this is our comfort. There is nothing that we can face that He has not experienced Himself. We can never believe that He does not care, because He truly knows how we feel. He also had no problem identifying with the undesirables - from the shepherds, to tax collectors and prostitutes. He came to be with those who needed Him most, God 'with' every person, whatever their status.

But '*Immanuel*' occurs elsewhere in Isaiah, in chapter 8 and verses 8 and 10. Here it is not a name but a cry of trust, from a nation facing humiliation and defeat; it is a yell, 'God is With Us!'. Immanuel is our comfort but can also be our battle cry.

Take counsel together, but it will come to nothing;
Speak the word, but it will not stand,
For God is with us (Immanuel).
Isaiah 8:10

Whatever we face, He, our Immanuel, is truly with us. '*I will never leave you nor forsake you*' is His promise (Hebrews 13:5). We too can cry 'God is with us'! Our protector and defender stands victorious in heaven, but also lives within us by His Spirit. We never have to face anything without Him.

Ask Yourself: *Does it comfort me that Jesus suffered as a human being, or do I find it hard to accept that He understands what I am going through?*

Ask God: *Show me Jesus, how and when to use 'Immanuel' as my battle cry.*

Pray: *Thank You Jesus that You are Immanuel, God With Us, in every sense of the word. You made Yourself as one of us in coming to live on earth. You are with me still, living within me by Your Spirit. Thank You that You promised to never leave me to face difficulties alone. I can stand in the face of hardship, knowing that the Victorious One stands with me. Almighty God is on my side, He is with me.*

Help me to take comfort from the fact that You know what it means to suffer and that You truly care and understand. Help me to trust You to fight for me and with me.

Amen

Further Reading: Matthew 1:18-25

DAY 21

SON OF DAVID

"Hosanna to the Son of David!
'Blessed is He who comes in the name of the LORD!'
Hosanna in the highest!"
Matthew 21:9

The genealogies in both Matthew 1 and Luke 3 show that Jesus was physically descended from King David. This was the fulfilment of the prophetic promise given to David through Nathan the prophet,

'And your house and your kingdom shall be established forever before you. Your throne shall be established forever'. (2 Samuel 7:16)

When the Angel Gabriel appeared to Mary he told her that her son, although the Son of God, would also be given David's throne,

'He will be great, and will be called the Son of the Highest; and the Lord God will give Him the throne of His father David.' (Luke 1:32)

The people of Jesus' time knew that the Messiah would

earn the title 'Son of David'. It is what the multitudes cried when they flocked to welcome Jesus as He rode triumphantly into Jerusalem (Matthew 21:9). As a descendant of David's royal line, in human terms He had a right to the throne of Israel. As they cried their hosannas they believed they were welcoming a king.

But why was it so important to God that Jesus was called the 'Son of David'? God chose David to be King of Israel, because he was '*a man after His own heart*' (1 Samuel 13:14).

David was far from perfect, but held a special place in God's affection, and knew a closeness with God that was ahead of his time. He was obedient to God, sought His will and direction, submitting himself to God's care and protection. David was a warrior King who brought peace to Israel and established a strong Kingdom. But He was also a worshipper, giving us many of the Psalms, establishing 24/7 worship in the Tabernacle, and overseeing the return of the Ark of the Covenant to Jerusalem. Jews of Jesus' time would have looked back and revered both David and his reign.

And then the 'Son of David' appeared. I believe David was a picture of Christ, albeit an imperfect one. Jesus was a man whose heart was completely and perfectly after God's heart, He lived His life in submission and obedience, a life that worshipped God. Our warrior king, He would fight, to the point of giving up His life, in order to establish a new and eternal kingdom. David brought the Ark, the presence of God back into the heart of the kingdom of Israel. Jesus came to bring the presence of God into the heart of all who would receive Him.

David was a man after God's own heart; Jesus was the heart of God personified.

Ask Yourself: *Is my heart after God's heart? Even when I get things wrong, does my heart want to be after His?*

Ask God: *Show me Jesus, any areas of my life where my heart goes after things that are not of You.*

Pray: *Thank You Jesus, that Your heart was so completely in tune with the Father's heart. Thank you that You came to earth willingly, out of obedience to the Father's will, but also to show us how much the Father loves us. You lived a life that worshipped God and honoured Him.*

Help me to tune my heart into Yours, so that my life is lived after Your own heart, in every area of my life. Forgive me when I set my heart on things that are not pleasing to You. I want my life to reflect You and to be known as someone who loves and serves You well.

Amen.

Further Reading: Luke 2:1-20

DAY 22

STAR OF JACOB

A Star shall come out of Jacob;
A Sceptre shall rise out of Israel,
Numbers 24:17

When we think of the prophets of the Old Testament who prophesied about the Messiah, we might think Isaiah, or Malachi, Jeremiah or Zechariah. But did you know that an ungodly and self-serving false prophet of the god Baal was used by God to prophecy about His Son? Balaam, was his name, and if you don't know his story, it's worth a read (Numbers 22-24). Not least because it features a talking donkey!

I love that God used a man with ungodly intentions and put His own words into his mouth, frustrating his attempts to curse God's people. Balaam says in Numbers 24:7,

'I see Him, but not now; I behold Him, but not near; A star shall come out of Jacob: A sceptre shall rise out of Israel'.

In Eastern tradition the image of a star was well known to

refer to a great and illustrious ruler, especially used in conjunction with the sceptre. This prophecy of Balaam's had two fulfilments: the great King David who was yet to come, but looking much further ahead, it also pointed to King Jesus. It was very likely that this prophecy informed the wise men (Matthew 2:2). The appearing of a bright and unusual star in the sky that heralded the birth of a great new King set them on their journey to find and worship Him.

He would be the one who shone with brilliance, lighting the darkness, like a bright star in the night sky. His brilliance would become a guiding light, and a symbol of hope.

Turn to the book of Revelation and there you see Him as He is now (Revelation 1: 13-17), His face like the *'sun shining in all its strength'*. So glorious that John, the one who in life had been so familiar with the person of Christ that he had laid his head on His chest, fell flat on his face as if dead before Him. In Revelation 22:16, Jesus says,

"I am the Root and the Offspring of David, the Bright and Morning Star."

No more a baby in a manger, no more a humble man, He stands as the brilliant glorious resurrected and ascended King, the Star of Jacob shining for all eternity.

Ask Yourself: *How do I feel about God using an ungodly man to prophecy about the Messiah? Or about Him speaking through astrology to magicians from the East?*

Ask God: *Show me, Jesus, when I have failed to hear You speaking, or failed to see what You are doing, because of prejudice.*

Pray: *Thank You Jesus, that You are the Star of Jacob - the promised King that carries the sceptre forever. Thank You Father that You used the words of the most unlikely prophet, and a sign in the heavens to bring the Magi to Bethlehem. Thank You that their willingness to make that journey, and the rich gifts that they brought, tell us so much about how special Jesus was at His coming. Thank You, Jesus, that You shine in brilliant glory in heaven now, and one day I will see You, just as John did.*

Help me to listen for Your voice, Father, and to know how to hear You. Thank You that I have Your word to guide me, and to use as a test for what I believe You are saying. Help me to be willing to be obedient to Your Word.

May the favour of Your face shine on me and my loved ones this Christmas.

Amen.

Further Reading: Matthew 2:1-14

DAY 23

CONSOLATION OF ISRAEL

DAY 23

CONSOLATION OF ISRAEL

And behold, there was a man in Jerusalem whose name was Simeon, and this man was just and devout, waiting for the Consolation of Israel,

Luke 2:25

There is a little story in Luke's gospel that introduces us to Simeon. Simeon was an old man, a devout lover of God who had waited for years for the promised Messiah. He was led to be in the Temple by the Holy Spirit at just the moment that Jesus' parents arrived with the infant Christ, and got to hold his Messiah in his arms and to prophesy over Him (Luke 2:25-35).

Luke tells us that Simeon was waiting expectantly for the '*Consolation of Israel*'. Now the word 'consolation' can be translated as 'comfort', 'help' or 'encouragement' and that is great. At the time of Jesus' birth, Israel was in dire need of comfort, help and encouragement and it was no wonder that Christ was longed for. He is the bringer of comfort. Elsewhere in scripture we are promised the comfort of His Holy Spirit (Acts 9:31), the comfort of the Scriptures (Psalm 119:50) and the comfort of God Himself (Romans 15:5).

But a more exact translation of the word 'consolation' is 'advocate': it has legal implication. It speaks of one ready to stand by your side before the judge and to give evidence on your behalf. Applying this meaning of consolation to the person of Jesus makes much more sense. Yes, He would be the bringer of comfort, but He was also coming as an advocate.

He stands today as our advocate before the Great Judge, His Father. He is our great High Priest (Hebrews 4:14 -16). What a comfort it is to picture Him standing beside us before God. When we know we need someone to speak on our behalf, because we mess up so easily. What a consolation to our troubled spirits, when guilt and shame threaten, to know that He gave His life, so that we can be free of those once and for all. He is our great encourager, our consolation, our advocate.

Ask Yourself: *Am I slow to take things to Jesus when I feel guilty or ashamed? Is that what God wants – for me to carry guilt or shame?*

Ask God: *Show me, Jesus, where I have held on to guilt and shame and not come to You for forgiveness. Or when I have been slow to accept that forgiveness, or to forgive myself.*

Pray: *Thank You Jesus, that You are my consolation. Thank You for the comfort that Your Word brings Me, and that Your presence brings me. Thank You that You are my advocate in heaven. Thank You that I can bring my mistakes to You and ask for forgiveness, and that You defend me, because Your blood covers all my sin.*

Help me to be quick to repent when I have failed You, and quick to let go of the guilt and shame you died to free me from.

Thank you that we no longer have to wait expectantly for You to come, but that You have come, and now live in our hearts. Thank You that we can look with expectancy for Your second coming, knowing that You will come to make all things new.

Amen.

Further Reading: Luke 2:21-40

DAY 24

JESUS

"And she will bring forth a Son, and you shall call His name JESUS, for He will save His people from their sins."
Matthew 1:21

Why was Jesus given the name Jesus? Well because that was the name God chose for Him! We know this because He told both Mary and Joseph, independently, through the words of their angel messengers, that Jesus was to be his name (Matthew 1:21, Luke 1:31). And Jesus is what they named Him, on the occasion of His circumcision. '*His name was called JESUS, the name given by the angel before He was conceived in the womb*' (Luke 2:21).

God didn't leave His Son's name to chance or to the will of men. It is interesting that the God who allowed Adam to name all the animals, made sure that He, and He alone, named His Son. In fact 'Jesus' might have been a popular choice. It would not have been an uncommon name of the time; we know of at least two other Jesus' mentioned in the New Testament.

Names in the Jewish tradition are important and it would have been so in Jesus' time. The name a child was given was believed to endue them with character traits, or to reflect what they were to become. It was much more than a title and was believed to capture a person's true essence. The name God chose, Jesus, is the Greek version of the Hebrew 'Joshua', or in full 'Jehoshua'. And it means 'Yahweh is Salvation'.

When you look up the word 'salvation', or 'Yeshuah' in the Hebrew Old Testament, it speaks of deliverance from harm, protection, help, victory, security. It is even translated in some places as 'welfare' or 'prosperity'.

The Angel told Joseph that Jesus would *'save His people from their sins'*. That is indeed what Jesus came to do. Through His death and resurrection He would provide a way for people to be saved from the consequences of sin - eternal separation from God the Father. But the idea of salvation in the Scriptures is not of a once and for all occurrence. We could say 'Jesus saved me' and look back to a specific moment when we submitted our lives to Him. But the Psalmist talks of God *being* His salvation (Psalm 62:7) and also asks Him to *be* his salvation (Psalm 79:9). Salvation is a past, present and future thing.

Jesus has the power to save us, by offering us forgiveness through His once and forever sacrifice. We come to Him in faith, believing He died and rose again. We ask Him to forgive us and become the Lord of our lives, and we are 'saved' (Romans 10:9-10). But we also continue to live in that salvation, in the sense that He still provides deliverance, protection, security, help and victory for us. And one day, in the future, our salvation will be complete. Sin and death will be no more, and all the things that cause us pain in this life will no longer have any power over us (1 Corinthians 15:54-55, Revelation 7:16-17). Jesus is our eternal salvation and we will know complete victory in Him.

***Ask Yourself**: Have I ever asked Jesus to be my Saviour? If I have, have I made Him Lord of my life? Am I living in the reality of His salvation.*

***Ask God**: Help me, Jesus, to make this Christmas all about You, to make you Lord of all that I do in celebrating Your birth.*

***Pray:** Thank You Jesus, that You fully embodied the name that God chose for You. Thank you for being my salvation, past, present and future. Thank You that I can look to You for protection, deliverance, help and victory in every area of my life on earth. Thank You that my salvation will be fully perfected in heaven.*

Thank You for Christmas and that every year we have the opportunity to remember Your coming to earth. Thank You that You came to bring salvation, not just to me, but to any who will believe on Your name. Help me to keep You at the centre of all things as we celebrate Your birth. Help me to tell others about just how amazing a Saviour You are. Thank You Jesus.

Amen.

Further Reading: Isaiah 9:6-7

REFLECTION

Which of the previous six descriptors of Jesus has impacted you most?

How has your heart and mind been illuminated afresh to see Jesus in a greater way than you have before?

What is the biggest personal challenge that you have taken from this section of devotionals?

Jesus, Son of God, Son of David, Star of Jacob, You came straight from the Father's heart to a world that needed You. You came to be our comfort and our consolation. You came to show us just how much You loved us. You came to be our Saviour, now and for eternity. This season is all about You, and we open up our hearts to You this Christmas, thanking You for revealing to us more of who You are. More than a baby in a manger, worshipped by shepherds and kings, You are God incarnate, King of Kings, Lord of Lords.

We worship you with our very lives.

Thank you Jesus

LOVE INCARNATE

He has many Names
And the greatest of all is Love.
Love came down at Christmas, love all lovely, love divine.
Love. He is Love.

Love planned it all before the beginning of time.
Love clothed Himself with human flesh.
Love humbled Himself and crept silently, yet powerfully, into a troubled world.

Love took a willing girl and grew within her. Love spoke to a troubled man and calmed him to obedience. Love drew shepherds in wonder and kings in worship.

Love challenged hatred, fear, shame and oppression.
Love opened His arms wide and embraced a world yet to know Him, giving all of Himself.

Love that was, and is and ever more will be. Love that saves, redeems, restores and sustains. Love that embraces us still, every day and into eternity.

Love came down at Christmas.
Wonderful Love, we embrace you, we bow in reverence before You, we worship You, we give ourselves to You.

ACKNOWLEDGEMENTS

Producing this devotional has been a new departure for me, so different from the fiction I have published before. I do believe, with the help of the Holy Spirit, that all I write, both fiction and non-fiction, carries biblical truth and points to Jesus and His Kingdom. But to put my pen to paper, or fingers to keyboard to be more accurate, to write a purely devotional book, was something of a dream. One that I am blessed beyond measure to see become a reality. I am no theologian, but I deeply love and revere the Word of God. It is my place of refuge, my source of strength, and where I meet with God each day. And in the Bible I meet the One who is the Word of God personified; He is there in it all.

So here it is. My thanks goes to the team at Kevin Mayhew for agreeing to publish this work for me, for catching the vision behind it, and for all of their invaluable help in bringing the book to print.

Thank you to all those who read it in the early stages of its existence, for your comments and your encouragement. Thanks especially to Joy Velykorodnyy, and to those who so kindly reviewed the book and were happy to have their endorsements added to it. You were such a gift when I badly needed encouragement to see this project to completion.

I am so grateful for my family and friends who have continued to support me in my writing journey. For those who have prayed for me and with me, through the struggles involved in bringing a book like this to fruition. But my greatest thanks as always goes to the One who has made it all possible. Jesus - may this book, and all that I write, give you the honour and glory that you are due.